RACING CARS

Frances Ridley

Editorial Consultant – Cliff Moon

RISING ★ STARS

Helping Everyone Achieve

nasen
NASEN House, 4/5 Amber Business Village, Amber Close,
Amington, Tamworth, Staffordshire B77 4RP

Rising Stars UK Ltd.
22 Grafton Street, London W1S 4EX
www.risingstars-uk.com

Every effort has been made to trace copyright holders and
obtain their permission for use of copyright material. The
publisher will gladly receive information enabling them to
rectify any error or omission in subsequent editions.
All facts are correct at time of going to press.

Published 2006

Cover design: Button plc
Cover image: The Photolibrary Wales/Alamy
Illustrator: Bill Greenhead
Technical artwork: IFA Design
Text design and typesetting: Nicholas Garner, Codesign
Technical adviser: Mark Rendes
Educational consultants: Cliff Moon and Lorraine Petersen
Pictures: Alamy: pages 4, 5, 8, 9, 12, 14, 15, 20, 22, 25, 31,
32, 34, 37, 38. Motoring Picture Library/NMM: pages 5, 7,
9, 10, 11, 13, 14, 19, 20, 21, 23, 24, 25, 26, 27, 31, 32, 33,
34, 35, 36, 37. Getty Images: pages 6, 19, 31, 33, 36, 37

British Library Cataloguing in Publication Data.
A CIP record for this book is available from the British
Library.

ISBN: 1-905056-94-X

Printed by Craft print International Ltd,Singapore

Contents

Racing cars

There are lots of different motor races.

Different kinds of cars race in them.

Le Mans cars race all day and all night.

They are fast and **reliable**. They must keep going for 24 hours without breaking down.

The Bentley Speed 8

Formula One cars take corners very fast.

They grip the track well.

The Renault R25

World Rally Cars race on tarmac, gravel and snow.

They are fast and very **stable**.

The Subaru Impreza

The 24 Hours of Le Mans

Le Mans is a town in France.

It holds a 24-hour race each year.

The first Le Mans was held in 1923.

The Le Mans start

Le Mans drivers used to run to their cars from the other side of the track.

This was stopped after 1969 as it wasn't safe.

The Le Mans Circuit has many famous landmarks.

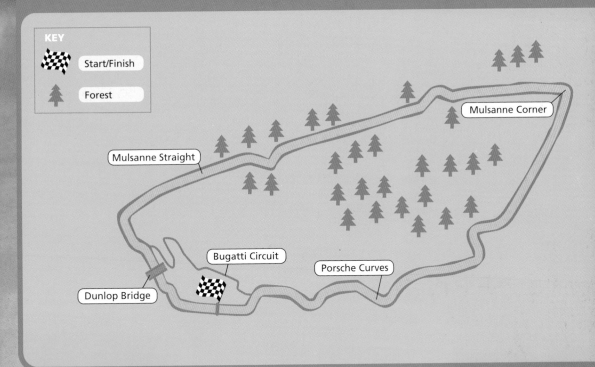

KEY

Start/Finish

Forest

Mulsanne Corner

Mulsanne Straight

Bugatti Circuit

Porsche Curves

Dunlop Bridge

The Le Mans circuit is 8.5 miles long.

It is mostly made up of country roads that have been closed off.

The car that does the most laps in 24 hours is the winner.

Le Mans cars

Top speed is important in a Le Mans car.

The Peugeot 905 racing at Le Mans in 1992

Speed record

The top speed record at Le Mans was set by Roger Darchy.

In 1988 he drove a WMP88 Peugeot at Le Mans.

It got to 251.7mph along the Mulsanne Straight.

Top teams since 1923

Bentley
5 Le Mans winners
in the 1920s

Alfa Romeo
4 Le Mans winners
from 1931 to 1934

Ford
4 Le Mans winners
from 1966 to 1969

Ferrari
9 Le Mans winners
since 1949

Jaguar
7 Le Mans winners
since 1951

Porsche
16 Le Mans winners
since 1970

Ford GT40

Ford wanted to race a car in Le Mans.

It tried to buy Ferrari in 1963 but Ferrari didn't want to sell.

So Ford made its own Le Mans car – the GT40.

Fast Facts!	
Top speed	165 mph
0-60 mph	5.5 seconds
Engine type	V8

In 1966 the GT40 won
Le Mans and beat Ferrari!

The GT40 won the next three
Le Mans.

In 1969 it beat the Porsche 908
by a few seconds.

In 1970 the new Porsche 917
won Le Mans and the glory
days of the GT40 were over.

Porsche 917

Porsche made the 917 in only ten months.
The first model was lightweight and powerful,
but it wasn't **stable**.

So Porsche changed the car's shape.
The new shape was much more stable.

The 917 won Le Mans in 1970 and 1971.

Porsche had raced cars at Le Mans since 1953, but the 917 was Porsche's first winner.

Audi R8

In 1999 the R8 raced in its first Le Mans. It came third.

It won Le Mans five times between 2000 and 2005.

The R8 is the most successful **LMP** car of all time.

Fast Facts!

Top speed	205 mph
0-60 mph	3.3 seconds
Engine type	**Turbo-charged V8**

Speed is not the only secret of the R8's success.

- It doesn't need to stop for petrol as often as other cars.

- Its engine has never let it down in a race.

- It can be **serviced** in record time.

Fixing the Morgan

(Part one)

Eddie sat on the bench. He had fixed the old Morgan's engine at last.

He felt happy but sleepy. He closed his eyes.

"Come on, Freddy!"

He woke with a jolt – a girl was pulling him across a road!

The Morgan was in front of them. But it wasn't old – it was new.

What was going on? This wasn't Grandad's garage!

The girl pushed him into the car.

"Come on, Freddy!"

She jumped in and started up. The car pulled out with a roar.

Eddie looked round.

There were lots of old cars – and they were all going at top speed!

"Where are we?" Eddie said.

"Gosh, Freddy!" said the girl. "What's up with you? This is Le Mans 1937!"

Continued on page 28

Formula One circuits

The Formula One Championship started in 1950.

It is run by the **FIA.**

F1 cars race on circuits. The circuits are in different countries. Each circuit is different.

The Monza circuit opened in 1922 and is the fastest F1 track. Monza is an Italian circuit.

Cars can average speeds of 126 mph here.

McLaren racing at Monza in 1997

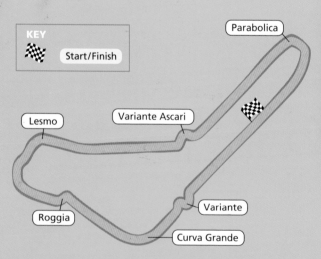

KEY

Start/Finish

Parabolica

Lesmo

Variante Ascari

Roggia

Variante

Curva Grande

The Monza circuit

Monte Carlo is the only F1 circuit that uses public streets.

The streets are closed for the race.

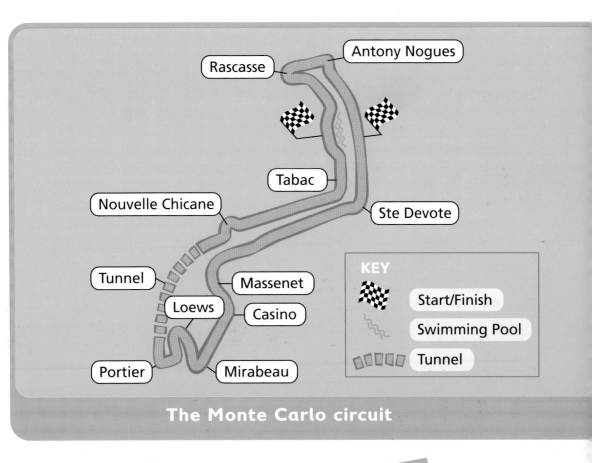

The Monte Carlo circuit

KEY

Start/Finish

Swimming Pool

Tunnel

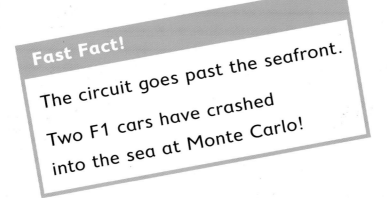

Fast Fact!

The circuit goes past the seafront.

Two F1 cars have crashed into the sea at Monte Carlo!

Formula One cars

Formula One car makers follow **FIA** rules.

The rules make the championship fair and safe. But each F1 team wants its car to be fastest.

The teams are always making changes to the cars. The FIA has to change its rules to keep up!

Monocoque

The Lotus 25 was the first **monocoque** car to win the championship.

Now all F1 cars are monocoque cars.

Skirts

Lots of cars in the 1970s had 'skirts'. Skirts made the cars very fast.

Many drivers were badly hurt or killed. The FIA banned skirts in the 1980s.

Cooper T51

The Cooper T51 was the first **mid-engined** car to win the F1 championship.

It didn't have a powerful engine but it was very fast.

Engine

Jack Brabham

Jack Brabham drove the T51 in the 1959 and 1960 World Championships.

He won the drivers' championship both times.

Cooper won the car-makers' championship both times.

Then other F1 teams started putting the engine behind the driver.

The Cooper car company didn't win any more championships. It closed in 1968.

Lotus 79

The Lotus 79 was based on the Lotus 78.

The Lotus 78 was a 'wing' car that had 'skirts' on both sides.

The skirts helped to suck the car to the ground. This was called 'ground effect'.

The Lotus 78 was the fastest car in the 1977 World Championship but it didn't win.
Its engine wasn't reliable.

Lotus 79 racing years	1978-79
Number of races	26
Number of wins	6

Mario Andretti

The Lotus 79 had a much better engine and it won six Grands Prix in 1978.

Mario Andretti won the drivers' championship.

Lotus won the car-makers' championship.

Williams FW14B

Nigel Mansell won the 1992 World Championship.

It was a great year for him.

Mansell won the first five races.

He won nine races during this championship — this was a record.

The car Mansell won in was the Williams FW14B.

The FW14B had a Renault V10 engine. This engine was powerful but didn't use much fuel.

The FW14B also had **active-ride suspension**.

This made the car very fast.

Team Facts!	
FW14B racing years	1992
Number of races	32
Number of wins	17

Fixing the Morgan

(Part two)

The Morgan was small but it was nippy.

The girl drove very fast.

"Come on, Pat," she muttered. "You can do it, girl."

"Pat?" said Eddie.

"Yes," said the girl. "What is it?"

So that was her name.

"Nothing," said Eddie. "You're driving well."

"Gosh, Freddy!" said Pat. "You must have been hit on the head. You never say things like that – I'm your sister, remember?"

But she had gone pink. She was happy that he'd said it.

Eddie was right – she did drive well.

She had a lot of guts and she handled the car well.

But the race wasn't over yet ...

Continued on page 40

WRC rallies

The World Rally Championship started in 1973.

It is run by the **FIA**.

Each rally event is different.

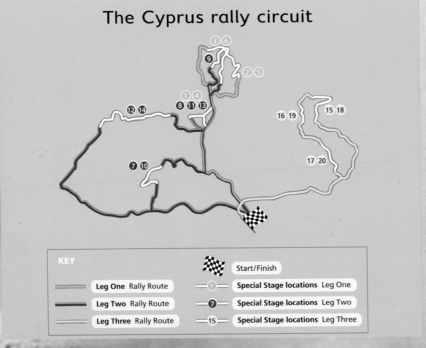

The Cyprus rally circuit

KEY

Start/Finish

Leg One Rally Route — Special Stage locations Leg One
Leg Two Rally Route — Special Stage locations Leg Two
Leg Three Rally Route — Special Stage locations Leg Three

The Cyprus rally has lots of bends. The cars race on sandy tracks and steep roads.

The first Monte Carlo rally
was in 1911.

The first WRC Monte Carlo
rally was in 1979. The cars
drive on narrow roads.

The fastest rally is in Finland.

The cars drive on loose,
smooth gravel.

There are lots of jumps.

The Swedish rally is cold
and snowy.

The cars use studded tyres.

Rally cars

Rally car makers have to follow **FIA** rules.

In the 1980s there were Group A and Group B cars.

The Ford RS200 Group B rally car

Group B cars were fast and powerful.

There were lots of crashes. Group B racing was stopped in 1986.

In 1997 World Rally Cars started racing.

World Rally Cars are faster than Group B cars, but they are much safer.

This is the Citroën Xsara T4 WRC

Citroën won the car-makers' championship from 2003 to 2005.

Sebastian Loeb won the drivers' championship in 2004 and 2005.

Audi Quattro SWB

The Audi Quattro was a Group B rally car.

It was the first rally car to have four-wheel drive.

Four-wheel-drive cars had always been very heavy.
People didn't think they were good for racing.

Audi used glass fibre to make the Quattro.
The car was lightweight and it handled
well. It was a great rally car.

Stig Blomqvist drove the Quattro in the 1980s.

He won the drivers' championship in 1984.

Audi won the car-makers' championship in 1982 and 1984.

Fast Facts!

Top speed	154 mph
0-60 mph	5.0 seconds
Weight	1303 kg

Mitsubishi Lancer Evolution V

The Lancer Evolution was a Group A rally car.

Mitsubishi raced its first Evo in 1993.

Tommi Mäkinen drove the Evo V in 1998 and Mitsubishi won the car-makers' championship.

Mäkinen won the WRC drivers' championship three times in the Evo V.

This 1999 Evo T is named after Tommi Mäkinen.

Fast Facts!

Top speed	147 mph
0-60 mph	4.7 seconds
Weight	1436 kg

The Lancer Evolution series are all World Rally Cars.

The Mitsubishi Lancer Evolution VIII

Lancia Delta HF Integrale

Lancia has won eleven World Rally Championships.

Six of these were won by the Lancia Delta Integrale.

No other car has won as many World Rally Championships.

Fast Facts!

Top speed	140 mph
0-60 mph	3.2 seconds
Weight	1232 kg

Lancia won the car-makers' championship from 1987 to 1992.

No other company has won six times in a row.

The Delta HF Integrale has wide wheel arches and a wide front bumper.

The front bumper looks good but it does an important job, too.

It gives more space to take in air — this helps to cool down the powerful engine.

Fixing the Morgan

(Part three)

It was Eddie's turn to drive.

He had driven Grandad's old Morgan but he had never driven it this fast!

"Get a move on!" said Pat.

Eddie felt better when he had done a few laps – but he still wasn't as fast as Pat.

Pat was mad by the time it was her next shift.

"We've lost loads of laps!" she said. "You're not yourself today."

It was dark, but Pat still drove at top speed.

She overtook other cars before Eddie even saw them.

Eddie drove even slower on his next shift.
It was so dark!

"Drive faster!" shouted Pat.

He put his foot down. The car roared. It felt great!

"Freddy!" shouted Pat.

There was a car in front.

Eddie pulled at the steering wheel and the Morgan crashed into a bush!

"Now you've done it!" said Pat.

Continued on the next page

Eddie lifted the bonnet and looked at the engine. He smiled.

"I can fix this!" he said to Pat.

"But you're rubbish with engines, Freddy!" she said.

Eddie got to work.

It didn't take long.

"It's done!" he said to Pat.

"Freddy, that's great!" said Pat. She kissed his cheek.

It was Eddie's turn to go pink.

Pat did most of the driving after that.

"The engine is running much better," said Pat. "What did you do to it?"

"Oh, this and that," said Eddie.

He felt happy but sleepy. He closed his eyes.

He woke with a jolt.

Grandad was shaking his arm.

"It's lunchtime," said Grandad. "Been having a nap?"

"Er, something like that," said Eddie.

Quiz

1 How many hours is the Le Mans race?

2 What was the 'Le Mans start'?

3 How many times did Bentley win Le Mans in the 1920s?

4 What was the nickname of the Porsche 917/20?

5 Name the fastest F1 circuit.

6 How many F1 drivers have crashed into the sea at Monte Carlo?

7 Name the first monocoque car to win the F1 Championship.

8 What car did Mansell drive in the 1992 F1 Championship?

9 Name the first rally car to have four-wheel drive.

10 Name the car that has won the most World Rally Championships.

Glossary of terms

active-ride suspension	A computer changes the car's suspension.
FIA	Fédération Internationale de l'Automobile. The FIA holds motor racing events and championships around the world.
flat 12	Engine with 12 cylinders laid flat.
landmarks	Places that stand out.
LMP	An LMP car is just made for high-speed racing at Le Mans.
mid-engined	Engine in the middle – behind the driver.
monocoque	Base frame and body are made from one piece.
reliable	Won't break down easily.
serviced	Checked and repaired.
stable	Won't roll over easily.
turbo-charged	A way of making an engine more powerful.
V8	Engine with 8 cylinders in a V-shape.

More resources

Books

Racing Cars, Ian Graham, Designed for Success Series, Heinemann Library (0-431-16569-6)
This book looks at how racing cars are made. It looks at racing car design and tells you how racing car engines work.

Into the Red: 22 Classic Cars that Shaped a Century of Sport, Nick Mason and Mark Hales, Virgin Books (1-852-27202-3)
Nick Mason drives 22 cars round Silverstone – and reading this book is like being there with him! The book comes with a CD of engine sounds.

Magazines

Autosport Magazine, Haymarket Publishing
A monthly magazine about motor racing.

Motorsport News, Haymarket Publishing
A weekly newspaper about motor racing.

Websites

http://news.bbc.co.uk/sport1/hi/motorsport
BBC website –Motorsport
Information and news about all kinds of motor racing.

http://www.racingsportscars.com
This website has lots of photos of different racing cars and races.

DVDs and Videos

The World's Greatest Rally Cars (2001) (Cat. No. DMDVD4301)
British rally driver Colin McRae looks at the cars that have shaped the world of rallying.

Le Mans (1971) (Cat. No. PHE8326)
This film stars Steve McQueen. It is one of the best racing films ever made. Much of the film was shot at Le Mans.

Answers

1   24 hours

2   The drivers ran across the track to their cars.

3   5

4   The Pink Pig

5   Monza

6   2

7   The Lotus 25

8   The Williams FW14B

9   The Audi Quattro SWB

10 The Lancia Delta HF Integrale

Index